Mommy and Me Cookbook

Recipes For Kid Size Ovens

Kristen Joyal 7-2?-02

Featuring recipes created for the
Easy Bake Oven™,
Barbie™ Bake With Me™ Oven,
the Mrs. Fields™ Baking Factory
or even your own full-size oven.

Cookbooks Available From:
Straight Forward Technologies
Wichita, KS 67204
316-207-3211 or 877-766-8566

Copyright 2002 Straight Forward Technologies

Written and edited by Kristen Joyal

Photographs by GS Memory Maker, Valley Center, KS

Cover art and design by Layne Johnson,
www.laynejohnson.com

Inside illustrations by elementary students from
Valley Center, Kansas

Printed in the United States by Instantpublisher.

Dash, Pinch and Smidgen measuring spoons manufactured by
World Kitchen.

ISBN 0-9718515-0-6
Library of Congress Number 2002090580

The publisher has made every reasonable effort to ensure
that the recipes in this book are safe when instructions included are followed, adult supervision is provided and manu-
factures recommendations are followed. The publisher does
not assume any responsibility for injury or damage caused
or sustained while performing the activities in this cookbook.
Terms mentioned in this book that are known to be trade-
marks are so indicated by the use of the trademark symbol.

Table of Contents

◆ ◆ ◆ ◆ ◆ ◆ ◆ ◆ ◆ ◆ ◆ ◆

Introduction

◆ ◆ ◆ ◆ ◆ ◆ ◆ ◆ ◆ ◆ ◆ ◆

I am happy to share with you, recipes that have been especially created for children to use in their small light bulb ovens.

My daughter Ashlyn received her first Easy Bake Oven™ for Christmas when she was three years old. It was only a few days after Christmas that we had already used all of the mixes that the manufacturer had supplied with her oven. Instead of buying more, we began to experiment with some of my Grandmother's family recipes. We were delighted with how well the small portions worked in her oven. We eventually purchased all three kid-size light bulb ovens that were on the market, so that we could try the recipes in each oven. We hope that you will enjoy baking these recipes in your own oven.

Kristen Joyal

Kitchen Cupboard Checklist

◆ ◆ ◆ ◆ ◆ ◆ ◆ ◆ ◆ ◆ ◆

Here is a list of some great items to have on hand
so that you are ready to BAKE!!

ITEM	✓	ITEM	✓
Sugar		Brown Sugar	
Vanilla Extract		Baking Soda	
Baking Powder		Cream of Tartar	
Chocolate Chips		Marshmallows	
Peanut Butter		Butter or Margarine	
Applesauce		Graham Crackers	
Oil		Rice Cereal	
Pretzels		Cinnamon	
Sprinkles		Eggs	
Butter Flavored Shortening		Dried Egg Whites (Expensive but great)	
Wax Paper		Plastic Bags (For Storing Mixes)	

Abbreviations used in this book.
T. = tablespoon   t. = teaspoon   c. = cup

Reminders

◆ ◆ ◆ ◆ ◆ ◆ ◆ ◆ ◆ ◆ ◆

- Adult supervision is recommended in the preparation of these recipes. Many recipes will require contact with hot pans and food. Please follow all manufacturers instructions.

- Cooking times for recipes are approximate and may vary depending on the oven, wattage of the light bulb and how long the oven was preheated.

- Remember to always remove the pan handling tool from the oven. Unfortunately we found out what happens to the tool when it is left in a hot oven.

- If you would like to bake these recipes in a normal full-size oven, pre-heat the oven to 350°. Baking times in the full-size oven will be approximate to those found with each recipe, although baking times can vary depending on the portion size you are baking.

- Always wash your hands before and after you start working with a recipe.

- If eggs are handled while preparing a recipe, it is also a good idea to wash your hands before handling any other food items.

- Some recipes call for the baking pan to be greased and floured. This may not be needed, depending on the condition of your pans and the manufacturer.

- If you are using the measuring spoons provided with this cookbook, then $\frac{1}{8}$ t. = dash, 1/16 t. = pinch and 1/32 t. = smidgen.

- The abbreviations used in this book are T. = tablespoon, t. = teaspoon and c. = cup.

GREAT ways to learn math while baking with your child.

As a math teacher, I am constantly looking at ways that I can help my own children learn to think mathematically. As parents we can help our children tremendously by showing them that math is fun and a part of everyday life. Below you will find some easy ways to incorporate math while you are baking with your children.

1. While preparing a recipe, ask your child how many cookies it takes to make a dozen, two dozen or whatever amount is appropriate to their age level.
2. Have your child experiment with your measuring spoons. Using water, have them determine how many $\frac{1}{2}$ teaspoons it will take to make 1 teaspoon. How many tablespoons are in a cup? You can devise so many different questions for them, all the while they will be having a great time playing with the water.
3. Explain what it means to double or triple a recipe. Then ask your child how much of each ingredient in a specific recipe they would need if they doubled or tripled the recipe.

4. While waiting for your recipe to bake, you can work with your children on the concept of time. Depending on the age of your child you could do one of the following:

a. How long is a minute? Set a kitchen time for a minute so your child can see just how long a minute is. Set the timer again, this time count with your child to see if you can count to 60 before the timer goes off. Explain that there are 60 seconds in a minute.

b. For older children you can work on the fractional parts of an hour. If there are 60 minutes in 1 hour, then how many minutes are in $\frac{1}{2}$ of an hour? How many minutes are in a $\frac{1}{4}$ of an hour?

5. While preparing a recipe you can ask your child questions such as:

a. If we make six cookies and we both get the same number of cookies, how many will we each get?

b. If I eat one of the six cookies, and then we split the rest, how many cookies will you get? This is a great chance to explain fractions. You might even want to take the 5 cookies and have your child divide them into two piles to show that you will each get 2 $\frac{1}{2}$ cookies.

Notes:

Cookies

Alan's Patriot Peanut Butter Football Cookies

Alan loves the New England Patriots. He loves peanut butter and he loves football. Alan helped develop this recipe so we let him decide what we would name it.

Ingredients:

$\frac{1}{4}$ c. Flour

2 $\frac{1}{2}$ T. Sugar

2 T. Butter or Shortening

$\frac{1}{2}$ Egg or Egg Substitute

1/16 t. Baking Soda

2 $\frac{1}{2}$ T. Brown Sugar

$\frac{1}{4}$ t. Vanilla

2 T. Peanut Butter

1. Combine all ingredients.
2. Put enough batter into a greased and floured baking pan so that it covers the bottom of the pan.
3. Bake for approximately 10 minutes or until golden brown.
4. Makes 4 baking pan size cookies.

Alan Joyal, Age 6

Snowball Sugar Cookies

These cute cookies are one of Ashlyn's favorite cookies. Since we don't get much snow in Kansas, we have to enjoy these "snowballs" on those cold winter days.

Ingredients:

3 T. Powdered Sugar	1/8 t. Baking Soda
2 T. Butter	1/8 t. Cream of Tartar
5 T. Flour	1/8 t. Vanilla

1. Combine all ingredients.
2. Roll dough into small balls.
3. Roll each ball in powdered sugar.
4. Bake for approximately 10 minutes.
5. Makes 1 dozen cookies.

Hanna Shelton
Age 6

Red, White & Blue Sprinkle Cookies

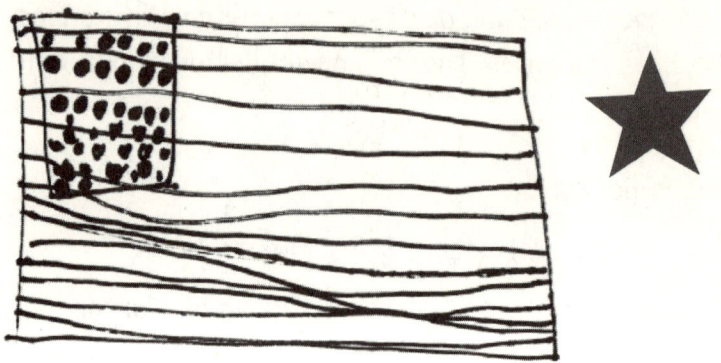

Ingredients:

2 T. Butter or Shortening   1 T. Sugar

3 t. Brown Sugar $\frac{1}{4}$ c. Flour

1/8 t. Cream of Tartar   1/8 t. Baking Soda

Red, White and Blue Sprinkles   2 t. Vanilla

1. Combine all ingredients.
2. Drop by teaspoons into a greased and floured baking pan.
3. Bake approximately 7 minutes.
4. Immediately press sprinkles on top of each cookie.

Hanna Shelton, Age 6

Sweet As A Rose
Oatmeal Fruit Cookie

My Grandmother Rose Marks use to make these cookies after she became a diabetic. I think you will find that they are GREAT even if you can have sugar.

Ingredients:

$\frac{1}{4}$ c. Flour   2 T. Butter or Margarine

$\frac{1}{4}$ t. Baking Soda $\frac{1}{4}$ c. Oatmeal

$\frac{1}{4}$ c. Water $\frac{1}{2}$ t. Vanilla

$\frac{1}{4}$ c. Raisins $\frac{1}{2}$ Egg or Egg Substitute

$\frac{1}{4}$ t. Cinnamon

1. Combine all ingredients.
2. Spoon dough into a greased and floured baking pan until the bottom is covered.
3. Bake approximately 10 minutes.

Emily Warner, Age 6

Angel Kiss Cookies

Ingredients:

2 T. Butter or Shortening

1 T. Brown Sugar

1/8 t. Baking Powder

¼ t. Baking Soda

¼ t. Vanilla Extract

1 T. Sugar   ¼ c. Flour

1 t. Water   Chocolate Chips

1. Combine all ingredients.
2. Drop by teaspoons into a greased and floured baking pan.
3. Place one chocolate chip on each cookie.
4. Bake for 10 to 12 minutes.
5. Makes 1 ½ dozen small cookies.

Krystal Partridge
Age 6

Oohey Gooey Friendship Cookies

It is hard to believe that only four ingredients can make these tasty cookies. It only makes one big cookie at a time, because the dough spreads out so much. There are no eggs in the recipe, so you know what that means, we can lick the bowl.

Ingredients:

2 T. Melted Butter $\frac{1}{2}$ c. Oats

$\frac{1}{4}$ c. Brown Sugar $\frac{1}{4}$ t. Baking Powder

1. Combine all ingredients.
2. Spoon dough into a greased and floured baking pan.
3. Spread to cover the bottom of the pan.
4. Bake for 10 to 12 minutes.

Hanna Shelton, Age 6

Monkey Banana Cookies

Ingredients:

½ Banana (Mashed)   4 t. Vegetable Oil

2/3 c. Oats   1/3 t. Vanilla

1/3 c. Raisins   1 T. Flour

1. Combine all ingredients.
2. Drop by teaspoons into a greased and floured baking pan.
1. Bake for approximately 10 minutes or until golden brown.
2. Makes 1 dozen cookies

David Chandler, Age 7

18

Lemonade Drop Cookies

Easy, Fast and Delicious –- you can even add to the lemon taste by adding ½ tablespoon of lemon zest if you crave that great lemon taste.

Ingredients:

¼ c. plus 1 T. Flour	1 ½ T. Vegetable Oil
3 T. Sugar	¼ t. Lemon Juice
¼ t. Baking Powder	¼ t. Vanilla
1 t. Water	

1. Mix all ingredients together in a mixing bowl.
2. Drop by teaspoons into a greased and floured baking pan.
3. Bake for approximately 10 minutes or until golden brown.

Alan Joyal, Age 6

Cookie Cutter Cookies

This is a great dough to cut out into your favorite shapes. All you need to find is some great miniature cookie cutters.

Ingredients:

2 T. Oats	1 T. Butter or Margarine
3 T. Flour	$\frac{1}{2}$ T. Honey
1/16 t. Baking Soda	1 T. Milk

1. Combine all ingredients.
2. Using floured hands roll out and then cut into the desired shape.
3. Bake for approximately 10 to 12 minutes.

Chris Fattig, Age 5

Irresistible Chocolate Chip Cookies

Grab your glass of milk and enjoy these wonderful chocolate chip cookies. What a great snack to make after school.

Ingredients:

1 t. Egg Substitute

1/32 t. Salt

2 T. Brown Sugar

1 t. Vanilla

1 T. Water

2 T. Flour

2T. Chocolate Chips

1. Combine all ingredients.
2. Drop by teaspoons into a greased and floured baking pan.
3. Bake for approximately 10 minutes or until golden brown.
4. Makes 2 baking pan size cookies.

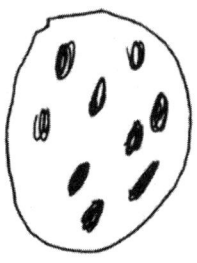 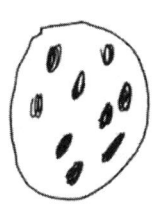 

Jessie Owens, Age 6

Sweet as Sugar
Tea Party Cookies

Little girls love to have a tea party. This is a great cookie to decorate with all your fancy sprinkles and favorite frosting. Don't forget the tea!

Ingredients:

½ Egg or Egg Substitute   ½ c. Flour

2T. Plus 1 t. Vegetable Oil   1/8 t. salt

½ t. Baking Powder   4 T. Sugar

2T. Water

1. Combine ingredients.
2. Drop by teaspoons into a greased and floured baking pan.
3. Bake for approximately 10 to 12 minutes.
4. Makes two dozen small cookies.

Options:
1. After cookies are cooled, frost and then sprinkle with your favorite sprinkles.
2. Press dough into the baking pan to create a cookie crust. Makes three cookie crusts.

Campfire Cookies

Use your imagination, and this cute cookie will remind you of a campfire.

Ingredients:

Vanilla Almond Bark (Cut or grated into small pieces with the help of an adult)

2 drops red or yellow food coloring

Chow Mein Noodles

1. Place small pieces of almond bark in baking pan.
2. Place in the oven until almond bark is melted.
3. Remove from oven.
4. Pour into a small bowl.
5. Stir in the food coloring.
6. Stir in the chow mein noodles.
7. Drop by teaspoons onto wax paper.
8. Cool and then serve.

Illustration by Dustin Warner

Crispy Vanilla Chip Cookies

Ingredients:

2 T. Shortening or Butter	¼ c. Flour
1/8 t. Baking Soda	1 T. Sugar
2 ½ T. Brown Sugar	¼ Egg
¼ t. Vanilla Extract	1 t. Milk
¼ c. Vanilla Chocolate Chips	1/3 c. Oats

1. Combine all ingredients.
2. Drop by teaspoons into a greased and floured baking pan.
3. Bake for 10 to 12 minutes.

Bailey Osborn, Age 6

Chocolate Almond Delight Cookies

Ingredients:

2 T. Flour	2T. Brown Sugar
½ t. Vanilla	½ c. Almonds
¼ Egg	2 t. Chocolate Chips

1. Combine all ingredients.
2. Drop by teaspoons into a greased and floured baking pan.
3. Bake for 10 to 12 minutes.

Zach Maloney, Age 6, Kameron Moss, Age 6
and Paul Suhr, Age 6

Super-Duper Chocolate Chip Cookies

Ingredients:

3 T. Flour	2 T. Brown Sugar
1 t. Sugar	2 t. Butter
1 t. Water	1/8 t. Vanilla Extract
1 T. Chocolate Chips	1/8 t. Baking Powder

1. Combine all ingredients except chocolate chips.
2. Stir until smooth.
3. Stir in chocolate chips.
4. Drop by teaspoons into a greased and floured baking pan.
5. Bake for 10 to 12 minutes.
6. Makes 1 dozen cookies.

Alayna Samia, Age 5

Glitzy Sparkle Cookies

As with many of the different cookie recipes in this cookbook, you have the option of butter or shortening. If you decide to use shortening. The butter flavored variety makes a great choice.

Ingredients:

1 T. Butter or Shortening

½ T. Sugar

½ T. Brown Sugar

2T. Flour

1/16 t. Cream of Tartar

1/16 t. Baking Soda

Sprinkles, chocolate candy, or frosting

Krystal Partridge, Age 6

1. Combine all ingredients except for sprinkles.
2. Roll teaspoons of dough into small balls.
3. Place in a greased and floured baking pan.
4. Press sprinkles on top of each cookie if desired.
5. Bake for 7 minutes.
6. Makes 6 small cookies.

Strawberry Blossom Cookies

Ingredients:

1 ½ T. Shortening or Butter   3 T. Flour

2T. Brown Sugar   3 T. Oats

1/8 t. Baking Powder   ½ t. Water

Strawberry Jelly

1. Combine all ingredients except for jelly.
2. Roll teaspoons of dough into balls.
3. Place each ball into a greased and floured baking pan.
4. In the center of each ball, make a small indention.
5. Place a small amount of jelly in the center of each cookie.
6. Bake for 10 to 12 minutes.
7. Cool before serving.

Danielle Shirley, Age 5

Rainbow Raisin Cookies

Ingredients:

1 t. Flour	1 T. Oats
1 T. Sugar	1/8 t. Baking Powder
½ T. Butter	1/8 t. Vanilla
1 T. Raisins	

1. Combine all ingredients.
2. Drop by teaspoons into a greased and floured baking pan.
3. Bake for 10 to 12 minutes.

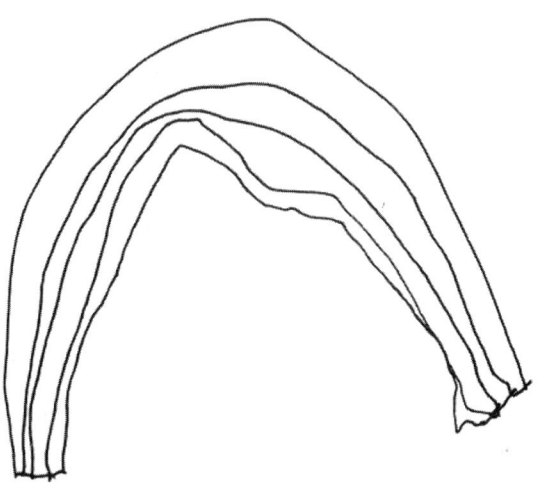

Jacob Glotta, Age 6

Notes:

Brownies, Pies and other Great Desserts!!

Rocky Road, Monster Truck Brownies

Ingredients:

¼ Egg or Egg Substitute   1 T. plus 1 t. Sugar

1/32 t. Baking Powder   1 T. plus 1 t. Flour

¼ t. Unsweetened Cocoa   1/8 t. Vanilla

1. Combine all ingredients.
2. Mix together until smooth.
3. Pour into a greased and floured baking pan.
4. Bake for approximately 15 minutes.

Alan Joyal, Age 6

Fruit Pizza Pie

This great dessert pizza is a blast to make, and even better to eat. Your family won't believe their eyes when they see what you have made for their dessert tonight!!!!!

Ingredients:

Sugar Cookie Recipe on Page 22
Whipped Topping
Pie Filling of Your Choice

1. Cover the bottom of a greased and floured baking pan with cookie dough.
2. Bake for approximately 10 minutes or until golden brown.
3. Let cool.
4. Spread whipped topping over the cooled cookie crust.
5. Spread pie filling on top of the whipped topping.
6. Top with spoonful of whipped topping.
7. Refrigerate until ready to serve

Oatmeal Pancake Bars

These pancake bars are not just for breakfast, they make a great snack anytime of the day. What a great mixture of oatmeal, peanut butter and chocolate chips

Ingredients:

1 T. Brown Sugar	$\frac{1}{4}$ c. Oats
$\frac{1}{2}$ T. Brown Sugar	$\frac{1}{2}$ T. Butter
$\frac{1}{2}$ T. Pancake Syrup	$\frac{1}{2}$ T. Peanut Butter
1/16 t. Vanilla	1 T. Chocolate Chips

1. Combine all ingredients.
2. Press into a greased and floured baking pan.
3. Bake for 12-15 minutes.
4. Makes 2 to 3 cakes.

Alan Joyal, Age 6

Marshmallow Mud

This recipe was especially created by Ashlyn. She is always into the marshmallows and chocolate chips, so one day we melted them in her oven and then mixed it with some cereal. Be sure and watch so that the marshmallows don't get too high and make a mess in your oven.

Ingredients:

2 T. Rice Cereal	1 T. Chocolate Chips
5 Small Marshmallows	$\frac{1}{2}$ t. Butter

1. Place cereal in the bottom of a buttered baking pan.
2. Top with chocolate chips and marshmallows.
3. Bake for 5 minutes.
4. Remove from oven.
5. Stir slightly.
6. Drop by teaspoons onto wax paper.

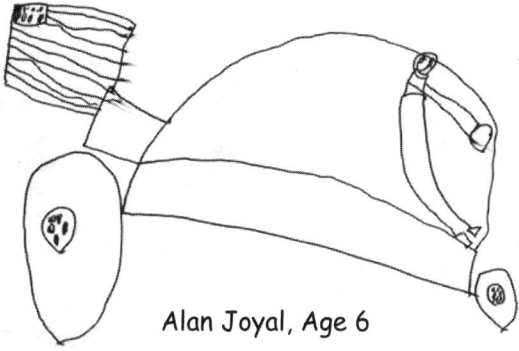

Alan Joyal, Age 6

Love Bug Cobbler

This is an easy, delicious recipe that will make a great dessert to share for a Valentine treat. Use the pie filling of your choice. Cherry pie filling looks great for Valentine's Day.

Ingredients:

Pie Filling	3 T. Flour
3 T. Brown Sugar	2 T. Butter
$\frac{1}{4}$ t. Cinnamon	2T. Sugar
1/16 t. salt	3 T. Oats

1. Place enough pie filling into the baking pan to cover the bottom.
2. Combine remaining ingredients in a small bowl and mix until crumbly.
3. Spoon mixture over pie filling and bake for 10 minutes.

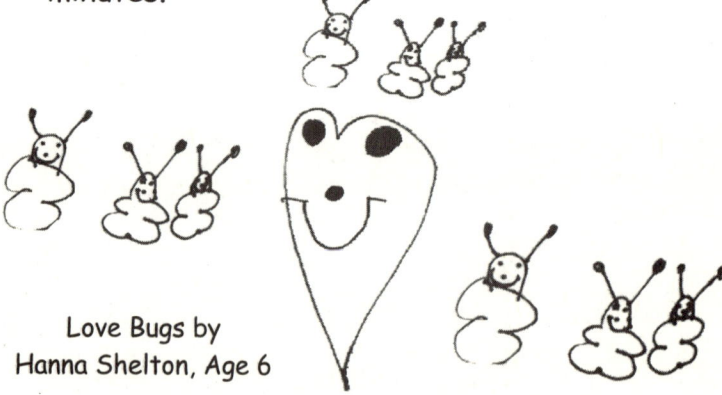

Love Bugs by
Hanna Shelton, Age 6

High in the Sky, Double Decker Pie

Ingredients:

2 Graham Crackers Smashed

¼ Chocolate Bar Smashed

5 Small Marshmallows

1 t. Butter melted

1. Mix graham crackers and butter together.
1. Press into a buttered pan to form the crust.
3. Place chocolate bar and marshmallows on crust.
4. Bake 5 minutes until chocolate and marshmallows are melted.

Brett Cox, Age 6

Pilgrim Pumpkin Pie

This pumpkin pie is made without a crust. I like to make this when I also plan to make a larger pie in my regular oven so that I do not waste any ingredients.

Ingredients:

2 ½ T. Pumpkin Pie Filling

2 T. Sweetened Condensed Milk

½ t. Pumpkin Pie Spice

1/16 t. Salt

Hanna Shelton—Age 6

1. Combine all ingredients.
2. Pour into a greased and floured baking pan.
3. Bake for 15 minutes or until the center is set.
4. Serve with whipped topping.

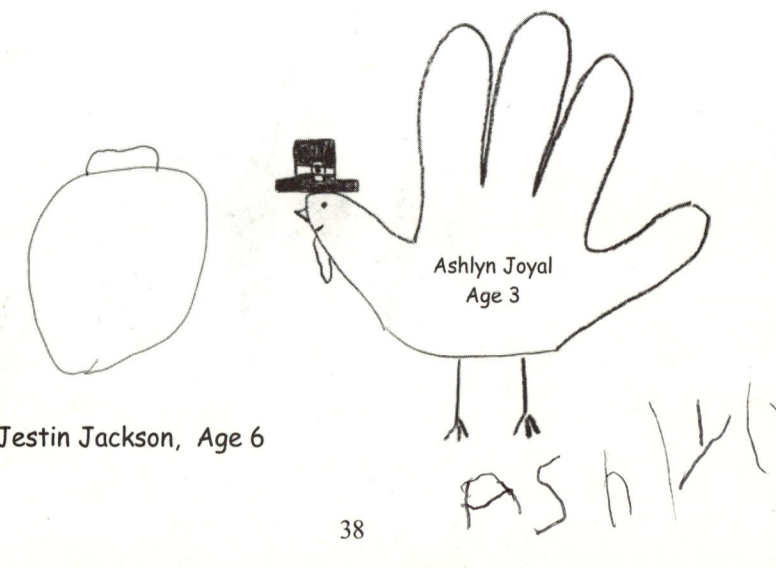

Ashlyn Joyal
Age 3

Jestin Jackson, Age 6

Itsy Bitsy Baby Smores

This is a variation of the famous and delicious smores that everyone likes to make around the campfire. This variation is so fast and easy you can make them any time you want.

Ingredients:

1 Sheet of Graham Crackers

8 Small Marshmallows

8 Chocolate Chips

1. Place half the sheet of graham crackers in the bottom of the baking pan.
2. Arrange marshmallows and chocolate chips on top of the graham cracker.
3. Bake in the oven for several minutes until the marshmallows and chocolate chips are melted.
4. Remove from the oven and put the other half of the graham cracker sheet on top to make a sandwich.

Darren Adwell, Age 7

Vanilla, Peanut Butter, Marshmallow Mess

Ohh!! What a yummy, delicious mess this recipe makes. Add chocolate chips or M&M's for a different variation.

Ingredients:

2 t. Vanilla Chips   4 Small Marshmallows

1 t. Peanut Butter   2 T. Rice and Corn Cereal

1. Place chocolate chips, peanut butter and marshmallows in a baking pan.
2. Bake for 3 minutes or until melted.
3. Remove from the oven
4. Pour melted mixture into the cereal and stir.
5. Drop by teaspoons onto the wax paper.
6. Cool and serve.

Emily Warner, Age 6

Peanut Butter Cup Dip

It never fails, we make this dip and it is not long before all the kids and adults around have gathered. Believe me, they won't leave until it is all gone.

Ingredients:

1 T. Peanut Butter   1 T. Chocolate Chips

Pretzels

1. Place the peanut butter in the bottom of a baking pan.
2. Sprinkle the chocolate chips over the peanut butter.
3. Heat in the oven for 5 minutes.
4. Remove from the oven and stir.
5. Serve with pretzels or even graham crackers.

Paul Suhr and Sara Russell, Age 6

Strawberry Cracker Pie

Submitted by Sandra Cox

Ingredients:

2 T. Sugar

2 Crackers Crushed

1/32 t. Baking Powder

Whipped Topping

1/8 t. Vanilla Extract

½ Egg White

¼ C. Strawberries

1. Combine all ingredients together except for strawberries.
2. Press mixture into a greased and floured baking pan to form a crust.
3. Bake 10 minutes or until bottom is golden brown.
4. Immediately remove shell from pan with a fork and then fill with strawberries.
5. Top with whipped cream if desired.

Beth Shirley and Hannah Powell, Age 5

Pudding Pie

This pudding pie can also be made with the sugar cookie crust recipe on page 22. Just cook the crust, cool and then fill with pudding.

Ingredients:

2 Graham Crackers Crushed

1 T. Melted Butter

2 T. Sugar

Prepared Chocolate Pudding

Whipped Topping

1. Place butter in the baking pan.
2. Place into the oven until the butter is melted.
3. Combine butter, sugar and graham crackers.
4. Press mixture into the baking pan.
5. Pour prepared pudding into the crust.
6. Top with whipped topping.
7. Refrigerate until ready to serve.

Cheyenne Yoakum-Moore, Age 5

Almond Bark Surprise

Oh what all you can do with a little melted almond bark. You can take almost anything, dip it in a little almond bark and make it look and taste great. A few sprinkles or chopped nuts will also add to that special sparkle.

Ingredients:

Chocolate or Vanilla Almond Bark—Grated or cut into small pieces with the help of an adult.

Choose One Ingredient Below:

Strawberries

Pretzels

Marshmallows

Walnuts, Peanuts or Pecans

Sprinkles or Chopped Nuts

1. Melt the almond bark in the oven.
2. Dip selected items into the melted almond bark.
3. Decorate with sprinkles. (Optional)
4. Place on wax paper to cool.

Triple Chocolate Brownie Pizza

Ingredients:

2 T. plus 1 t. Flour   2 T. Sugar

½ Egg or Egg Substitute   1 T. Butter

¼ c. Chocolate Chips   1/32 t. Baking Soda

1/8 t. Vanilla   M&M's

Coconut   Chocolate Syrup

1. Combine flour, egg, butter, chocolate chips, sugar, baking soda and vanilla.
2. Spoon into a greased and floured baking pan.
3. Bake for 18 to 20 minutes.
4. Cool
5. Spread a thin layer of chocolate syrup on top of the brownie crust.
6. Top with M&M's and Coconut.

Cheyenne Yoakum-Moore, Age 5

45

Out of This World Brownies

Ingredients:

2 T. Sugar

½ T. Unsweetened Cocoa

¼ Egg or Egg Substitute

1 T. Chocolate Chips

2 T. Flour

1 T. Vegetable Oil

1/16 t. Vanilla

1. Combine Ingredients.
2. Spoon into a greased and floured baking pan.
3. Bake for 18 to 20 minutes.
4. Cool and Serve.

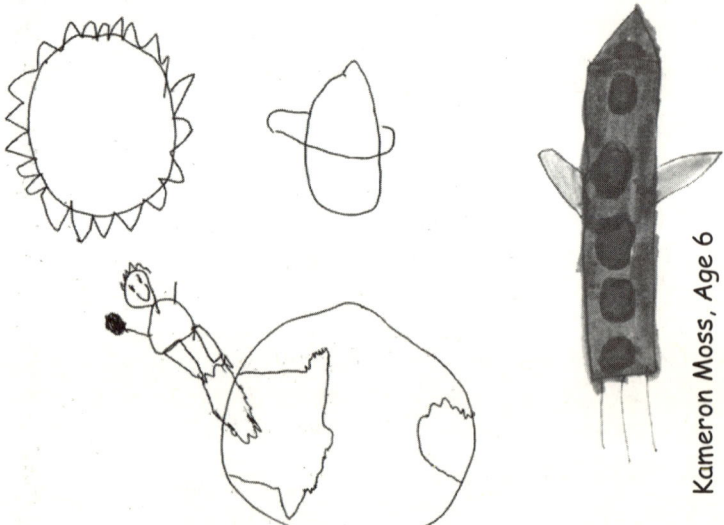

Jacob Huebert, 7 Years Old

Kameron Moss, Age 6

Butterscotch Haystacks

Ingredients:

2 T. Butterscotch Chips $\frac{1}{2}$ T. Peanut Butter

$\frac{1}{2}$ C. Flakes Cereal or Chow Mein Noodles

Peanuts

1. Combine the butterscotch chips and peanut butter in the baking pan.
2. Place in the oven until the chips are melted.
3. Pour the melted mixture over the cereal and peanuts.
4. Mix together.
5. Drop by teaspoons onto the wax paper.
6. Place in refrigerator until cool.

Devin Duerksen, Age 5

Peanut Butter Bars

Ingredients:

1 ½ T. Shortening	2 T. Brown Sugar
1/8 t. Vanilla Extract	1 T. Peanut Butter
1/8 Egg Substitute	¼ C. Flour
2 T. Chocolate Chips	1 T. Peanut Butter

1. Combine all ingredients.
2. Press batter into the bottom of a greased and floured baking pan.
3. Bake for 15 minutes.

These bars are so great, everyone will wonder when the next pan will be ready!

Jasmine Sanchez, Age 5

48

Rudolph's Carrot Muffins

If your family is like ours, we always have to leave some carrots out for the reindeer. Next year we are going to leave some of these great muffins for Santa and his reindeer.

Ingredients:

1 T. Brown Sugar	$\frac{1}{2}$ T. Oil
2 $\frac{1}{2}$ T. Grated Carrot	2 T. Flour
1/8 t. Cinnamon	1/8 t. Pumpkin Pie Spice
1/16 t. Baking Powder	1/32 t. Baking Soda
1 t. water	

1. Combine all ingredients.
2. Place muffin batter into the baking pan.
3. Bake for 12 to 14 minutes.

Reindeer by Hannah Shelton, Age 6
Carrot by Miles Balthazor, Age 6

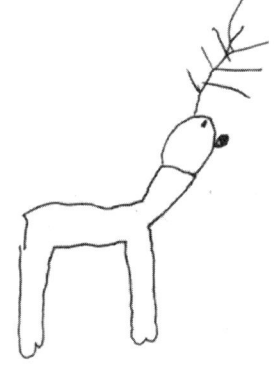

49

Icky, Sticky Cinnamon Rolls

Ingredients:

¼ c. Sugar   1 T. Cinnamon

2 T. Melted Butter   Refrigerated Biscuits

1. Combine sugar and cinnamon in a small bowl.
2. Cut each biscuit into four small pieces.
3. Dip each piece of biscuit into the melted butter and then into the sugar cinnamon mixture.
1. Place each piece of coated biscuit into a greased and floured baking pan.
2. Bake for 15 minutes.
3. Drizzle with your choice of frosting.

Alan Joyal, Age 6

Lady Bug Banana Bread

Ingredients:

1 T. Butter Flavored Shortening	2 T. Sugar
$\frac{1}{4}$ Egg or Egg Substitute	$\frac{1}{4}$ C. Flour
1/8 t. Baking Soda	1/16 t. Salt

$\frac{1}{4}$ Banana (Mashed)

1. Combine all ingredients.
2. Pour batter into a greased and floured baking pan.
3. Bake for 20 minutes.
4. Makes two baking pans of bread.

Alan Joyal, Age 6

Mini Cinni Muffins

Here is a great muffin that you can make the night before and serve to all your family for breakfast. Serve with a little butter and juice and you have a great breakfast treat.

Ingredients:

1/3 c. Raisin Bran Cereal

1 t. Oil

1 T. Flour

1 t. Baking Powder

1 T. Milk

$\frac{1}{4}$ Egg or Substitute

1 T. Brown Sugar

1/8 t. Cinnamon

1. Combine all ingredients.
2. Place muffin batter into a greased and floured baking pan.
3. Bake for 12 to 14 minutes.

Peanut Butter Calzone

One day we were testing a recipe that used refrigerated biscuits. We had to figure out something to do with the extra biscuits. We rolled a biscuit out and put a little peanut butter in the middle and folded it over and baked it. This is how the Peanut Butter Calzone was born. You can also add a few chocolate chips or marshmallows. We tried peanut butter and jelly, but the jelly leaked out and burned.

Ingredients:

1 Refrigerated Biscuit   1 or 2 t. Peanut Butter

Optional:

Marshmallows   Chocolate Chips

1. Press biscuit into a circle the size of the baking pan.
2. Place peanut butter in the middle of one half of the circle.
3. Fold the biscuit in half, sealing edges of the dough with your fingers.
4. Bake for 13 to 15 minutes or until golden brown.
5. Makes one calzone.

Polar Bear
Ice Cream Sandwich

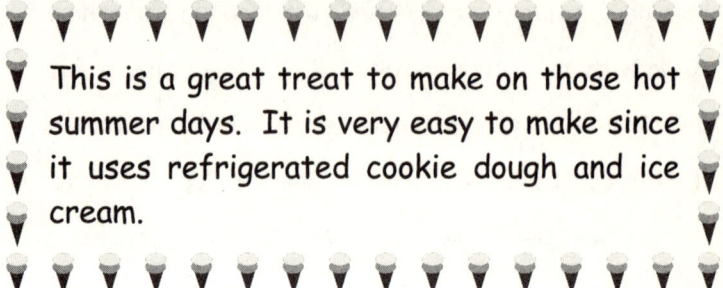

This is a great treat to make on those hot summer days. It is very easy to make since it uses refrigerated cookie dough and ice cream.

Ingredients:

Refrigerated chocolate chip cookie dough

Your favorite flavor of ice cream

1. Press a ½ inch slice of cookie dough into a greased and floured baking pan.
2. Bake for 12 to 14 minutes.
3. Have an adult remove the warm cookie from the pan.
4. Repeat the process to make another cookie.
5. When both cookies are cooled, spoon a small amount of ice cream onto the top of one cookie.
6. Place other cookie on top of the ice cream to create your sandwich.
7. Place in the freezer until ready to serve.

Birds Nest Surprise

Ingredients:

2 T. Coconut   1 T. Chocolate Chips

Jelly Beans   or Almond Bark

1. Place the coconut in the baking pan.
2. Place chocolate chips or shaved almond bark on top of coconut.
3. Bake in the oven for 5 to 7 minutes or until the chocolate is melted.
4. Remove from the oven.
5. Mix the coconut and the chocolate.
6. Spoon the coconut mixture onto wax paper and shape to resemble a bird's nest.
7. Fill with jelly beans.
8. Refrigerate until firm.
9. The almond bark will hold together better than the chocolate chips.

Notes:

Cakes

Hippity, Hoppity Carrot Cake

Ingredients:

3 T. Sugar	$\frac{1}{2}$ Egg or Egg Substitute
2 T. Oil	1/8 t. Baking Soda
1/8 t. Vanilla	$\frac{1}{2}$ t. Cinnamon
3 T. Flour	$\frac{1}{4}$ c. Grated Carrots
1 T. Walnuts	

1. Combine all ingredients.
2. Pour into a greased and floured baking pan.
3. Bake for 15 minutes.
4. Cool.
5. Top with Easter Bunny frosting.

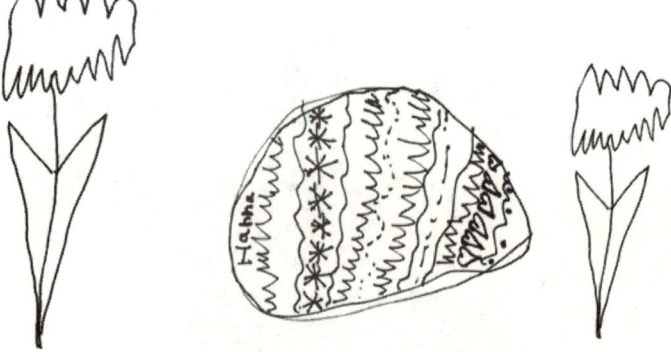

Flowers Illustrated by Allison Keeler, Age 6
Easter Egg Illustrated by Hanna Shelton, Age 6

Applesauce Cake

Ingredients:

2 T. Brown Sugar	1 T. Shortening
1/8 Egg Substitute (Optional)	2 T. Flour
2 T. Applesauce	1/8 t. Cinnamon
1/8 t. Pumpkin Pie Spice	1/8 t. Baking Soda
1 T. Raisons	

1. Combine all ingredients.
2. Pour into a greased and floured baking pan.
3. Bake for 20 minutes.
3. Makes 2 Cakes

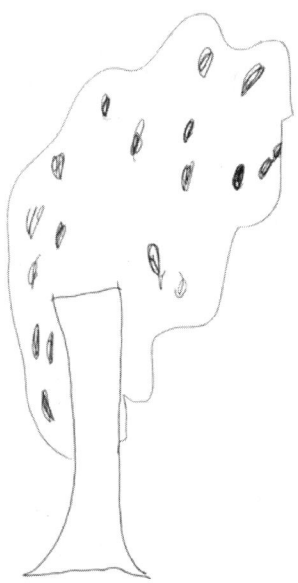

Frosting (Optional)
1 t. Melted Butter
2 T. Powdered Sugar
1/8 t. Vanilla
Water

1. Combine ingredients.
2. Add water until desired
   consistency is reached.
3. Pour over warm cake.

Alan Joyal, Age 6

Red Hot
Tea Party Cakes

Ingredients:

2 T. Flour	1/8 t. Baking Powder
1 t. Sugar	1 t. Butter or Shortening
2 t. Milk	1 t. Red Hot Candy

1. Combine flour, baking powder, sugar and butter in a small bowl.
2. Mix with a fork until the mixture is crumbly.
3. Stir in the milk.
4. Press into a greased and floured baking pan.
5. Arrange the red hot candy on top of the cake mixture.
6. Bake for 10 to 12 minutes.
7. Cool before serving.

Rainbow Cake

This is a perfect cake for any occasion. You can bake one to celebrate a birthday, any holiday or just for dessert tonight. Just add your favorite frosting and decorations and you will have a cake for any celebration.

Ingredients:

3 T. Flour	2 T. Sugar
$\frac{1}{4}$ t. Baking Powder	1/16 t. Salt
1 T. Butter	$\frac{1}{4}$ Egg or Substitute
1/8 t. Vanilla	1 $\frac{1}{2}$ T. Milk

1. Combine all ingredients.
2. Pour into a greased and floured baking pan.
1. Bake for 20 minutes.

Patrick Schrater, Age 5

61

Notes:

Baking Mixes!

Hey, now we can make our own baking mixes for our oven. Isn't that great!! Just make sure to tell Mom to store them in a cool dry place and they will last for a couple of months.

Oatmeal, Chocolate Chip Bar Mix

We absolutely love the different baking mixes that are in this cookbook. After preparing the mix, just store in an air-tight container or even a plastic storage bag. This is a great way for busy families to still enjoy their kid size ovens.

Ingredients:

1 1/3 c. Oats

½ c. Brown Sugar

½ c. Sugar

1 t. Baking Soda

½ c. Pecans or Walnuts

1 c. Chocolate Chips

1 1/3 c. Flour

1 t. Baking Powder

¼ t. Salt (optional)

1. Combine all ingredients.
2. Store in an air-tight container.

To make a bar:
1. Combine 1/3 cup of bar mix with 1 tablespoon melted butter, ½ teaspoon vanilla and 1 teaspoon water.
2. Press into baking pan.
3. Bake 10 to 12 minutes.

Flying High Chocolate Swirl Brownie Mix

Ingredients:

½ c. plus 2 T. Flour   2/3 c. Sugar

1/3 c. Unsweetened Cocoa   ½ c. Walnuts

2/3 c. Brown Sugar   ½ c. Choc. Chips

½ c. Vanilla Chocolate Chips ¾ t. Salt

1. Combine all ingredients.
2. Store mix in an air-tight container.

To make brownies:
1. Combine 1/3 cup brownie mix with ½ teaspoon vanilla, 1 tablespoon oil and ½ egg or egg substitute.
2. Bake for 15 minutes.

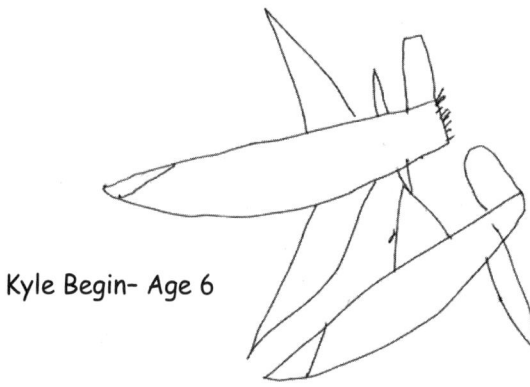

Kyle Begin– Age 6

Cocoa Mocha Brownie Mix

Ingredients:

1 2/3 c. Sugar   1 1/3 c. Flour

½ t. Baking Powder   ¼ t. Salt

¾ c. Cocoa   ¾ c. Chocolate Chips

1. Combine all ingredients.
2. Store in an air-tight container.

To make brownies.

1. Combine 1/3 cup brownie mix with
    1 teaspoon water, 1 teaspoon melted
    butter and ¼ teaspoon vanilla.
2. Pour into a greased and floured baking
    pan.
3. Bake for 15 minutes.

Ariel baking in
her oven.

Ariel Spillman, Age 6

Solar Blast Cookie Mix

Ashlyn Joyal
Age 3

Ingredients:

1 Packet Kool-aid Drink Mix

1 $\frac{1}{2}$ c. Vanilla Chocolate Chips

$\frac{1}{2}$ t. Baking Soda

1 c. Sugar

1 $\frac{3}{4}$ c. Flour

$\frac{1}{2}$ t. Baking Powder

1. Combine all ingredients.
2. Store in an air-tight container.

To make cookies:
1. Combine $\frac{1}{2}$ cup of the mix with 1 tablespoon of butter, 1 teaspoon vanilla and 2 teaspoons water.
2. Drop by teaspoons into a greased and floured baking pan.
3. Bake for 10 to 12 minutes.

Hot Chocolate Cake Mix

This cake mix is our favorite. The hot chocolate mix gives it just enough chocolate flavor. We like to put the mix in an air-tight storage container and just measure out how much we need.

Ingredients:

½ c. Sugar   1 Packet Hot Chocolate Mix

¾ c. Flour   ½ t. Baking Soda

¼ t. Salt   3 T. Shortening

1. Combine all ingredients.
2. Store mix in an air-tight container.
3. To prepare cake, mix 1/3 cup mix with 5 teaspoons water.
4. Bake for 15 minutes.
5. Frost cake with Hot Chocolate Frosting and serve.

Beth Shirley, Age 5

Hot Chocolate Frosting Mix

Ingredients:

2 c. Powdered Sugar

1 Package Hot Chocolate Mix

2 T. Instant Nonfat Milk Powder

2 T. Butter Flavored Shortening

1 T. Cocoa

1. Combine powdered sugar, hot chocolate mix and milk powder in a medium bowl.
2. Cut in shortening.
3. Store frosting mix in an air-tight container or in small storage bags.
4. Store in a cool dry place.

To make frosting.
1. Combine 1/3 cup mix with 2 teaspoons water.
2. Stir with a spoon until smooth.
3. Add additional water to reach desired consistency.

Will frost approximately 4 single layer cakes.

Dough Boy and Girl Biscuit Mix

Ingredients:

5 c. Flour	3 T. Baking Powder
1 t. Salt	¾ c. Shortening

1. Combine flour, baking powder and salt in a medium size bowl.
2. Cut shortening into the flour mixture.
3. Store mix in an air-tight container or divide among small plastic bags.

To make biscuits:
Combine
1 Cup Biscuit Mix
¼ to 1/3 Cup Milk
2 Tablespoons Butter or Margarine

1. Drop by teaspoons into a greased and floured baking pan.
2. Bake 10 minutes.
3. For a variation, add ¼ cup cheese to biscuit dough before baking.

Chocolate Pecan Cake Mix

Ingredients:

1 ¼ c. Flour	2/3 c. Unsweetened Cocoa
1 t. Salt	2 ¼ c. Sugar
½ c. Pecans	1 t. Baking Powder

1. Mix ingredients together.
2. Store in an air-tight container.

To make a cake:

1. Mix ½ cup of mix with 1 ½ tablespoons of melted butter and ½ egg or egg substitute.
2. Pour into a greased and floured baking pan.
3. Bake for 15 minutes.

Jessica Holdaway, Age 5

Super Easy
Pizza Crust Mix

****
You know those store bought pizza crust mixes. They can also double as a mix for your small light bulb oven. Just store the mix that is leftover in a labeled plastic storage bag. This way you can make your pizza and not waste any mix.
****

Ingredients:

Store bought pizza crust mix

Water

For one pizza crust:

1. Combine 2 tablespoons of crust mix with 3 teaspoons of water.
2. With floured fingers, press the dough into the bottom of a greased and floured baking pan.
3. Top with the desired ingredients and bake for 10 to 12 minutes or until bottom is golden brown.

Hope Watkins, age 6

Baby Cheetah Cookie Mix

Ingredients:

1/3 C. Flour	1/3 C. Oats
2 T. Sugar	2 T. Brown Sugar
2 T. Chopped Nuts	2 T. Chocolate Chips
2 T. Vanilla Chips	¼ t. Baking Powder
¼ t. Baking Soda	1/16 t. Salt

1. Combine all ingredients together.
2. Store in an air-tight container.

To make cookies:
1. Measure out ¼ cup of cookie mix and place in small bowl.
2. Add ½ tablespoon of butter, 1/16 teaspoon vanilla, ¼ teaspoon powdered egg white and ½ teaspoon water.
3. Mix together until the butter is mixed in well.
4. Drop by teaspoons into a greased and floured baking pan.
5. Bake for 10 to 12 minutes.

David Chandler, Age 7

Notes:

Frosting Recipes

Creamy Butter Frosting

Ingredients:

2T. Shortening   2T. Butter

2/3 c. Powdered Sugar $\frac{1}{2}$ T. Milk

$\frac{1}{4}$ t. Vanilla Extract   Water

1. Cream shortening and butter together.
2. Combine the creamed mixture and powdered sugar.
3. Add the milk and vanilla to the mixture.
4. Mix in small amounts of water until the frosting reaches the desired consistency.

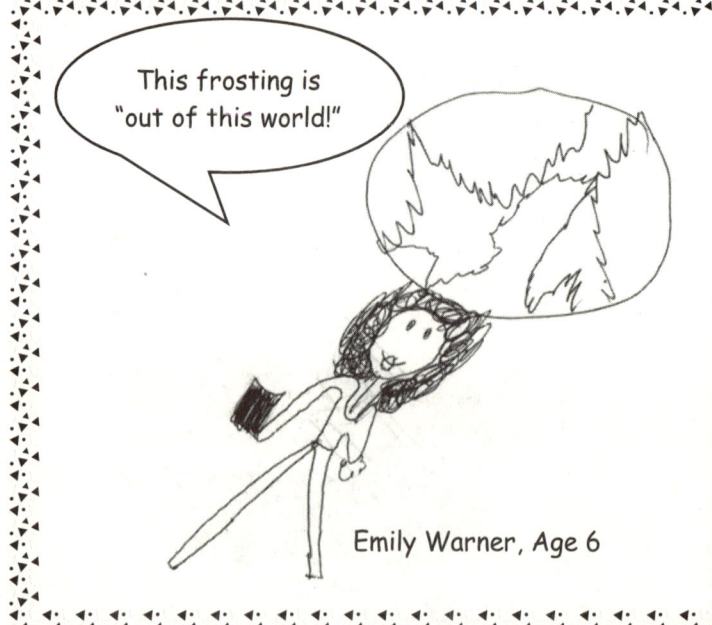

Emily Warner, Age 6

Rainbow Butter Frosting

Ingredients:

1 T. Butter   1 c. Powdered Sugar

1 T. Milk   1 t. Vanilla Extract

Food Coloring   Sprinkles

1. Mix the butter, powdered sugar, milk and vanilla together until smooth and creamy.
2. Add drops of food coloring until frosting is the desired color.
3. Frost cake or cookies.

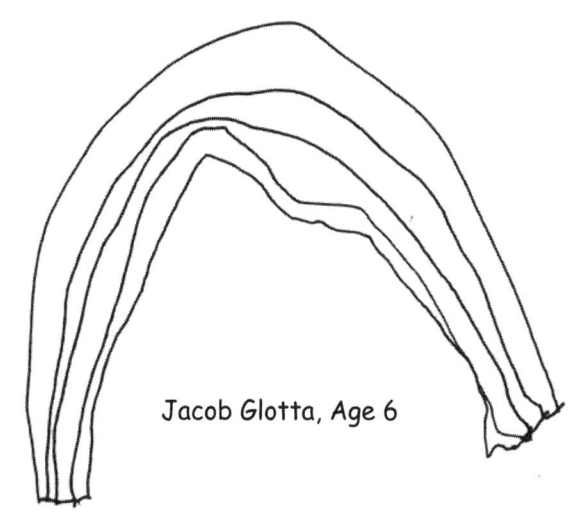

Jacob Glotta, Age 6

Easter Bunny Frosting

This tastes great on "Hippidy, Hoppidy Carrot Cake. Just keep your leftovers in the refrigerator.

Ingredients:

1/3 c. Sugar 1/8 Pkg. Cream Cheese

1 t. Butter $\frac{1}{4}$ t. Vanilla Extract

1. Combine all ingredients.
2. Mix until smooth and creamy.

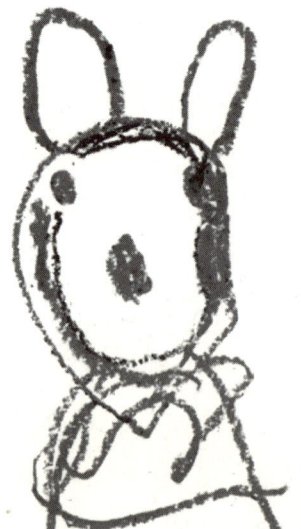

Evann Shelton, Age 3

Peanut Butter, Chocolate Chip Frosting

Ingredients:

2 T. Chocolate Chips	1 t. Peanut Butter
1 t. Butter	2 t. Corn Syrup
Water	

1. Combine the chocolate chips, peanut butter, butter and corn syrup in a mixing bowl.
2. Pour into a baking pan.
3. Bake until chocolate chips are melted.
4. Stir and add water to until it is the desired consistency.

Hanna Shelton, Age 6

Notes:

Great Snack Foods!

Hey Emily, what did you fix for our snack? Pizza, chips and dip or three pigs in the blanket?

Ham & Cheese Snacks

Ingredients:

Refrigerated Biscuits   1 T. Shredded Cheese

2 t. Ranch Salad Dressing

½ Slice Ham Lunchmeat—Cut Up

1. Press ½ biscuit into a greased and floured baking pan.
2. Spread salad dressing on top of the biscuit.
3. Top with ham and cheese.
4. Bake for 10 to 12 minutes until crust is golden brown.

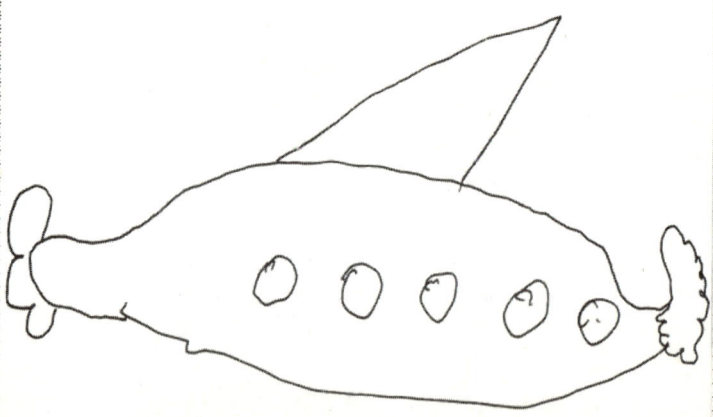

Meghan Palmer, Age 6

BBQ Pineapple Pizza

Ingredients:

Refrigerated Biscuits	1 T. Shredded Cheese
2 t. BBQ Sauce	1 T. Crushed Pineapple

½ Slice Ham Lunchmeat—Cut Up

1. Press ½ biscuit into a greased and floured baking pan.
2. Spread BBQ sauce on top of the biscuit.
3. Top with ham, cheese and pineapple.
4. Bake for 10 to 12 minutes until crust is golden brown.

Hanna Shelton, Age 6

Layered Taco Dip

Ingredients:

2 T. Refried Beans   1 T. Shredded Cheese

1 T. Sour Cream   Tortilla Chips

1. Spread refried beans in the baking pan.
2. Spread sour cream on top of the refried beans.
3. Top with shredded cheese.
4. Bake 2 to 3 minutes or until the cheese is melted.
5. Serve with tortilla chips.

Alan Joyal, Age 6

Three Pigs in a Blanket

Recipe by Sandy Cox

Ingredients:

1 Refrigerated Biscuit

3 Small Pieces of Hotdog

1 T. Shredded Cheese

1. On a lightly floured surface, press biscuit into a circle larger than the baking pan.
2. Place hotdog and cheese in the center of the biscuit.
3. Fold edges of circle towards the center, covering the hotdog and cheese.
4. Bake 12 to 14 minutes or until crust is golden brown.

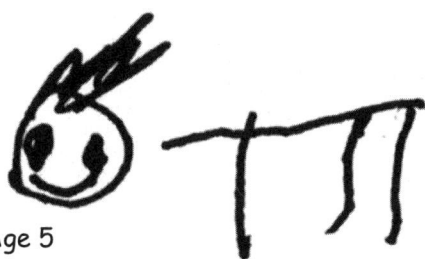

Devin Duerkson, Age 5

Pizza Chip Dip

Ingredients: *Recipe by Sheila Chiskowski*

2 T. Pizza Sauce   2 T. Cream Cheese

2 T. Shredded Cheese Tortilla Chips

1. Spread the cream cheese in the bottom of the baking pan.
2. Top with pizza sauce and then cheese.
3. Bake for 5 minutes or until cheese is melted.
4. Serve with tortilla chips.

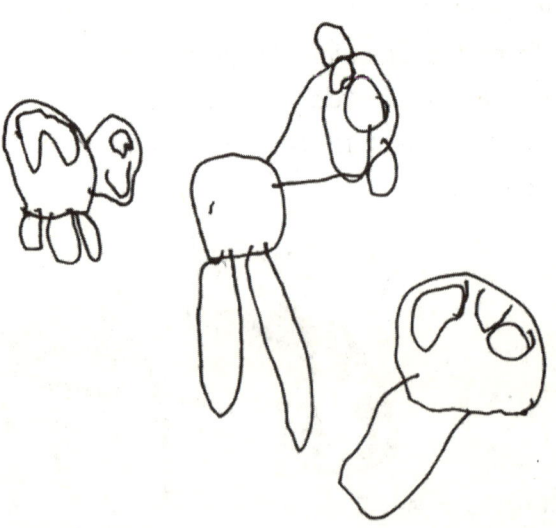

Crispy Cinnamon Crisps

Ingredients:

Flour Tortilla	Sugar
Cinnamon	Butter

1. Cut a tortilla so that it fits in a baking pan.
2. Cover the tortilla with a thin layer of butter.
3. Sprinkle the tortilla and butter with sugar and cinnamon.
1. Bake for 7 to 10 minutes until the tortilla is crisp.
2. Cool and serve.

Bailey Osborn, Age 6

Hot Diggidy Dog Pizza

This easy , delicious recipe will probably be one of your favorites. It combines two great American favorites, pizza and hotdogs.

Ingredients:

Refrigerated Biscuit   Hotdog—Cut in thin slices

1 T. Ketchup   1 T. Shredded Cheese

1. Press the biscuit into a greased and floured baking pan.
2. Spread ketchup over the biscuit.
3. Place the sliced hotdogs on top of the ketchup.
4. Top with shredded cheese.
5. Bake for 10 to 12 minutes until the biscuit crust is golden brown on the bottom.

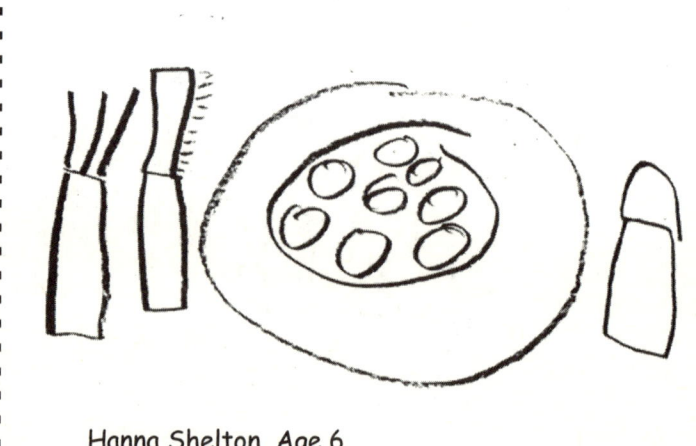

Hanna Shelton, Age 6

Cheese Calzone

This recipe is similar to the peanut butter calzone. Instead of a just a snack, you can serve the cheese calzone as a main course.

Ingredients:

Refrigerated Biscuit   2 t. Pizza Sauce

2 t. Shredded Cheese

1. Press the biscuit into a circle the size of the baking pan.
2. Spread pizza sauce in the middle of one half of the circle.
3. Top pizza sauce with cheese. Be sure and keep cheese away from the edge.
4. Fold the biscuit in half, sealing the edges of the dough with your fingers.
5. Bake for 13 to 15 minutes or until golden brown.
6. Makes one calzone.   Maxx Johnson, Age 6

Baked Spaghetti

This is a great recipe to make when you are already boiling some spaghetti for the rest of the family!

Ingredients:

2 T. Cooked Spaghetti   1 T. Spaghetti Sauce

1 T. Shredded Cheese

1. Place the spaghetti in the bottom of a buttered baking pan.
2. Pour spaghetti sauce over the spaghetti.
3. Top with cheese.
4. Bake for 5 to 7 minutes or until cheese is melted.
5. Serve.

Miles Balthazor, Age 6

Monkey Macaroni

Ingredients:

2 T. Cooked Macaroni

1 T. Shredded Cheese

1 t. Butter

1. Place macaroni in the bottom of a buttered baking pan.
2. Top macaroni with butter and cheese.
3. Bake for 5 to 7 minutes or until cheese is melted.
4. Stir to combine macaroni, cheese and butter.
5. Serve.

David Chandler, Age 7

Index

Cookies

Brownies, Pies and Other Desserts

Index

Brownies, Pies and Other Desserts (continued)

Cakes

Index

Acknowledgements

I would like to offer thanks to all the following people that worked so hard to help make this cookbook a reality.

To the students at Abilene Elementary who provided amazing art work for the recipe pages. I still smile as I thumb through the cookbook. A big thanks to Jamie Pearson for all her help and patience with this project.

To GS Memory Maker in Valley Center, Kansas for donating time and talent to help with the photographs that are included throughout the cookbook. It was your initial willingness to help that really sparked my enthusiasm.

To Layne Johnson, for his brilliant illustration of Ashlyn and for all his time and patience. I do not know what I would have done without your expertise and great ideas.

And finally to all my family and friends for the support I received throughout the duration of this project. You were all so willing to listen to my crazy ideas and my daily updates. I will never forget your kindness.

Kristen Joyal

Notes:

Mommy and Me Cookbook Published by:

Straight Forward Technologies
Roger and Kristen Joyal
Wichita, KS 67204
316-207-3211 or 877-766-8566
Email: info@straightforwardtech.com
www.straightforwardtech.com